MW01120851

# Invertebrates

Reviewed by Bill Houska, D.V.M.,
Ridgemont Animal Hospital, Rochester, New York,
and James K. Morrisey, D.V.M., Cornell University
School of Veterinary Medicine.

Debra J. Housel

# Table of Contents

What Is an Invertebrate?  . . . 3

Simple Invertebrates  . . . . . . . 8

Mollusks . . . . . . . . . . . . . . . . 14

Arthropods  . . . . . . . . . . . . . 18

Glossary  . . . . . . . . . . . . . . . . 23

Index . . . . . . . . . . . . . . . . . . . 24

blue crayfish ▶

There are more than
one million different
*invertebrates.*

2

# What Is an Invertebrate?

Swish, squirm, wiggle.  Creep, creep, crawl.

Most animals move, but many cannot move like you do.  You bend, run, hop, and climb. Some animals swish, squirm, wiggle, creep, or crawl.  Others can't move at all!

Of course, we're talking about *invertebrates* (in-VER-tuh-brits)—animals without backbones.

Invertebrates' bodies are much simpler than yours. Instead of brains they have a bundle of cells called a *ganglia* (gang-GLEE-uh). This controls their bodies just as your brain controls yours. But, since they lack brains, these animals cannot do many of the things that you can.

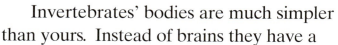

Invertebrates can be found in the air, under the water, and on the land. Some are *carnivores* (KAR-nuh-vohrs). They eat other animals. Ladybugs, for example, can eat 50 bugs a day!

Sea anemones ▶
eat other sea
animals.

◀ butterfly

5

## Would You Believe?

Invertebrates have rest periods, but they never fall asleep.

▲ Oysters eat the dead plant and animal matter found in the sea water.

Other invertebrates are *herbivores* (HUR-buh-vohrs), or plant eaters. Snails, for example, eat leaves, vegetables, and fruit.

Some invertebrates eat meat and plants. They are *omnivores* (OM-nuh-vohrs). Earthworms, for example, eat tiny pieces of rotting plants and animals found in the soil.

◄ Swarms of grasshoppers may eat every green thing for miles.

# Simple Invertebrates

You have a heart, stomach, and lungs. But not all animals have these organs. Sponges and coral do not.

Some invertebrates have soft bodies and a stinging body part. They use the sting for defense and to kill *prey*. If you've ever tangled with jellyfish, you know how much their stings hurt!

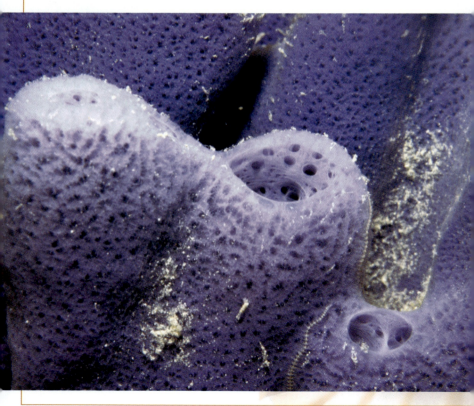

## Microscopic Life

Tiny one-celled animals, like bacteria, are invertebrates. But they're not what most people think of when they hear the word invertebrate. They are called *microscopic life* because you need a microscope to see them.

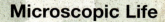
◀ blue sponge

▲ sea nettle

## Sponges

Sponges live in the ocean. Until 200 years ago, people believed that sponges were plants. Now we know that they are the most simple of all *multi-celled* animals.

9

▲ If a lost limb still has some of its body attached, it can grow into a new sea star such as the one above.

Can you see the buds on this coral? ▶

Some simple invertebrates can grow new body parts! A sea star has five limbs. If one of its limbs gets torn off, a new one grows. This is called *regeneration*.

Simple invertebrates *reproduce* in odd ways. Sponges, jellyfish, and coral do so by *budding*. Young start growing on their parents' outer bodies. When a baby gets big enough, it breaks off as a separate animal.

Did you know that every earthworm is both *male* and *female?* It's true!

When earthworms mate, they lay eggs into a structure like a cuff that grows around their bodies. When the earthworm moves, the cuff slides up until it goes over its head and makes a cocoon. In a few weeks, new earthworms hatch from the cocoon.

earthworm ▼

▲ Planaria are common flatworms. ▼

Most flatworms are *parasites*. They live on other animals' bodies. Some flatworms reproduce by splitting in two. One part has the head. The other has the tail. Each piece then grows the missing part. The pieces become two new flatworms.

# Mollusks

*Mollusks* (MOL-uhsks) have soft bodies. Most have shells covering them. Snails are mollusks with four feelers. The eyes at the tips of the two longest *tentacles* tell light from dark. A snail moves around using a *muscular* foot on the bottom of its body. This foot has *mucus* to help the snail glide across any surface.

▲ A thin, shiny trail shows where a snail has been.

### Aestivation

If the weather becomes hot or dry, a snail *aestivates* (es-tuh-VAYTS) so that it doesn't dry out. It sticks to a surface with its foot. It pulls the rest of its body into its shell. It stays like this until the conditions improve.

Clams live most of their lives under sand or mud. They pull water through their shells. This provides them with food and oxygen. Clams are *bivalves*. That means they have two shells. Their shells are *hinged* so they can open and close them.

After a young clam grows a shell, it buries itself. Each year it grows larger. If you look at a clamshell, you will see lines. Just as a tree stump has rings, the clamshell's lines mark the years of its life. You can tell its age by counting the lines on its shell.

**Amazing!**
Some clams can live for 20 years.

◀ clams ▲

The octopus and the squid are mollusks without shells. Both live in the sea. They grab other animals with their stinging tentacles and pull them into their mouths.

These animals move by shooting jets of water from their bodies. If attacked by a *predator*, they squirt ink. The dark cloud gives the squid or octopus a chance to get away.

### Smarty Pants!
The octopus is the smartest invertebrate and may actually be able to think.

◀ octopus

▲ The giant squid is the largest known invertebrate.

Little is known about the giant squid. A live one has never been caught. Scientists study the dead squids that wash ashore. The largest ever found was 60 feet long.

▼ **Just look how long a giant squid can be!**

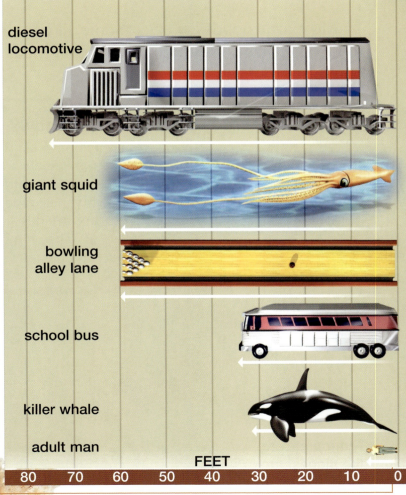

diesel locomotive

giant squid

bowling alley lane

school bus

killer whale

adult man

FEET

80   70   60   50   40   30   20   10   0

# Arthropods

You have leg joints. These joints let you move at the knee and ankle. Many invertebrates have jointed legs, too. These *arthropods* (AR-thruh-pods) include spiders, bees, lobsters, and crabs.

Most arthropods lay eggs. Some, like moths, go through stages. They change several times from birth to death.

▼ a desert centipede

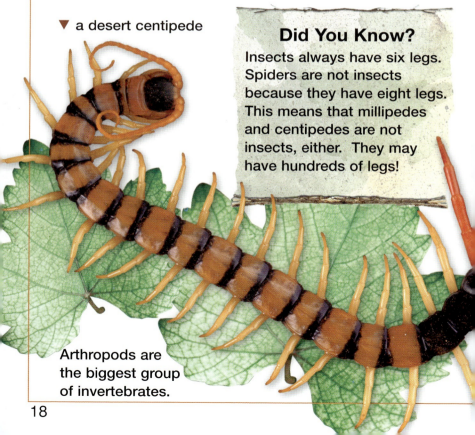

### Did You Know?

Insects always have six legs. Spiders are not insects because they have eight legs. This means that millipedes and centipedes are not insects, either. They may have hundreds of legs!

Arthropods are the biggest group of invertebrates.

## Mosquito Life Cycle

How does an arthropod's life go from beginning to end? Here is a mosquito's life from egg to adult.

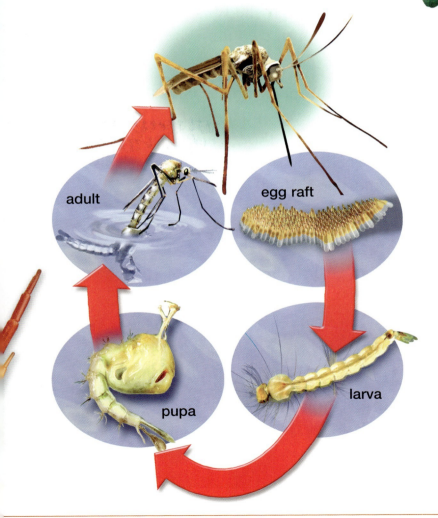

adult

egg raft

pupa

larva

You have a skeleton. It holds you up and gives you shape. Flesh covers your bones. Unlike you, arthropods have no bones. They have a hard covering on their outer bodies called an *exoskeleton*. To grow larger, an arthropod *molts*. It sheds its exoskeleton. Its body is unprotected until the new covering hardens.

Most arthropods' bodies have three *segments*. The head has eyes and a mouth. The next part is the *thorax*. The thorax often has legs and wings. The last part is the *abdomen*. This may have more legs, a tail, or a stinger.

▲ hermit crab

**Would You Believe?**

Insects, which are also arthropods, are the only animals that live everywhere—including Antarctica!

scorpion

▲ Some arachnids are poisonous.

Spiders, scorpions, and ticks are kinds of arthropods called *arachnids*. They have eight legs and are carnivores. Spiders build webs to catch bugs. Scorpions sting their prey. Ticks can get into your pet's fur and suck its blood.

*Crustaceans* (kruhs-TAY-shuhns) have hard outer bodies. They are crabs, shrimp, lobsters, and crayfish. Most crabs and shrimp live in the sea, but a few can be found in fresh water. Lobsters always live in salt water.

Crayfish look like small lobsters but live in fresh water. One kind actually lives on land. During the day, the chimney crayfish digs a hole in a swamp. It pushes up dirt, forming a "chimney." At night it comes up the chimney to look for food.

▲ chimney crayfish

Some people keep invertebrates as pets because they are quiet and don't need much care. They are also interesting to watch! It's fun to have a hermit crab, a crayfish, or an ant farm. Would you like a pet invertebrate?

# Glossary

**abdomen**   the hind (back) part of an arthropod

**aestivates**   rests during hot or dry conditions

**antennae**   long, thin body parts on the heads of some animals, used mainly for feeling

**arachnids**   eight-legged arthropods that eat other animals or their blood

**arthropods**   invertebrates with jointed legs and a hard outer structure, like a shell (exoskeleton)

**bivalves**   mollusks with hinged shells

**budding**   reproducing by growing young on a parent's outer body

**carnivores**   animals that eat only meat (other animals)

**crustaceans**   arthropods with hard outer shells and two pairs of antennae

**exoskeleton**   the hard outer cover of an arthropod, somewhat like a shell

**fertilize**   to provide what is needed for new life to begin

**ganglia**   a group of nerve cells that serve as an invertebrate's simple "brain"

**herbivores**   animals that eat only plants

**hinged**   having a joint or flexible part that allows two halves to move open and closed

**invertebrates**   animals without backbones (spines)

**microscopic life**   single-celled animals which can only be seen with a microscope

**mollusks**   soft-bodied invertebrates that usually have shells

**molts**   sheds (gets rid of) the exoskeleton (the hard outer cover)

**mucus**   a slippery, sticky, liquid-type substance that comes from living things

**multi-celled**   having many of the tiny parts called cells that make up living things

**muscular**   body tissue made of muscle that enables an animal to move

**omnivores**   animals that eat both plants and meat

**parasite**   a living thing that lives on other living things and gets its nourishment from them

**predator**   an animal that hunts, kills, and eats other animals

**prey**   any animal that is hunted by another for food

**regeneration**   the process of regrowing a lost body part

**reproduce**   to create more animals like oneself

**segments**   the individual parts of a thing that is divided

**tentacles**   long flexible body parts that are usually used for feeling and grasping

**thorax**   the second of the three main parts of an arthropod

# Index

aestivation . . . . . . . . . . page 14

ant. . . . . . . . . . . . . . . page 22

arachnid . . . . . . . . . . . page 21

arthropod . . . . . . . pages 18–22

bee . . . . . . . . . . . . . . . page 18

bivalves . . . . . . . . . . . page 15

butterfly . . . . . . . . . . . page 5

carnivore . . . . . . . . . . page 4

centipede . . . . . . . pages 18, 21

clam . . . . . . . . . . . . . . page 15

coral . . . . . . . . . pages 8, 10, 11

crab . . . . . . . . pages 18, 20, 22

crayfish . . . . . . . . . . pages 3, 22

crustaceans . . . . . . . . . page 22

earthworm . . . . . . . pages 7, 12

exoskeleton . . . . . . . . . page 20

flatworm . . . . . . . . . . page 13

ganglia . . . . . . . . . . . . page 4

giant squid . . . . . . pages 16–17

grasshopper . . . . . . . pages 6–7

herbivore . . . . . . . . . . . page 7

invertebrates . . . . . . . . page 3

jellyfish . . . . . . . . . . pages 8, 11

ladybug . . . . . . . . . . . . page 4

lobster . . . . . . . . . pages 18, 22

microscopic life . . . . . . page 9

millipede . . . . . . . . . . page 21

mollusks . . . . . pages 14, 16–17

mosquito . . . . . . . . . . page 19

moth . . . . . . . . . . . . . . page 18

octopus . . . . . . . . . . . . page 16

omnivore . . . . . . . . . . . page 7

parasite . . . . . . . . . . . page 13

planaria . . . . . . . . . . . page 13

regeneration . . pages 10–11, 13

reproduction . . . . pages 11–13

scorpion . . . . . . . . . . . page 21

sea anemone . . . . . . pages 4–5

sea nettle . . . . . . . . . . . page 9

sea star . . . . . . . . pages 10–11

shrimp . . . . . . . . . . . . page 22

snail . . . . . . . . . . . . pages 6, 14

spider . . . . . . . . . pages 18, 21

sponge . . . . . . . . pages 8, 9 11

tick . . . . . . . . . . . . . . . page 21